THE CHICAGO BLACKHAWKS

ANDREW LUKE

childsworld.com

Published by The Child's World®
800-599-READ • www.childsworld.com

Copyright © 2026 by The Child's World®
All rights reserved. No part of this book may be reproduced or utilized in any form or by any means without written permission from the publisher.

Photography Credits
Cover: ©Melissa Tamez/Icon Sportswire/Getty Images; multiple pages: ©Hanna Siamashka/iStock/Getty Images; GLYPHstock/iStock/Getty Images; md tauhidul/Shutterstock; page 5: ©Luke Hales/Getty Images; page 6: ©George Reinhardt/Corbis Historical/Getty Images; page 9: ©B Bennett/Getty Images; page 10: ©Michael Reaves/Getty Images; page 12: ©Michael Reaves/Getty Images; page 12: ©Michael Martin/NHLI/Getty Images; page 13: ©Derek Leung/Getty Images; page 13: ©B Bennett/Getty Images; page 14: ©Bill Smith/NHLI/Getty Images; page 16: ©Bruce Bennett Studios via Getty Images Studios/Getty Images; page 16: ©Minas Panagiotakis/Getty Images; page 17: ©Graig Abel/Getty Images; page 17: ©Focus on Sport/Getty Images; page 18: ©B Bennett/Getty Images; page 18: ©Bruce Bennett Studios via Getty Images Studios/Getty Images; page 19: ©Bruce Bennett/Getty Images for NHL/Getty Images; page 19: ©Jim McIsaac/Getty Images: page 20: ©Thearon W. Henderson/Getty Images; page 20: ©Michael Reaves/Getty Images; page 21: ©Candice Ward/Getty Images; page 21: ©Michael Reaves/Getty Images; page 22: ©Melchior DiGiacomo/Getty Images; page 23: ©Focus on Sport/Getty Images; page 25: ©Chris Williams/Icon Sportswire/Getty Images; page 26: ©Rick Stewart/Allsport/Hulton Archive/Getty Images; page 29: ©Steve Babineau/NHLI/Getty Images

ISBN Information
9781503870703 (Reinforced Library Binding)
9781503871892 (Portable Document Format)
9781503873131 (Online Multi-user eBook)
9781503874374 (Electronic Publication)

LCCN
Library of Congress Control Number: 2024950264

Printed in the United States of America

ABOUT THE AUTHOR

Andrew Luke is a former journalist-turned-freelance writer. He has written about everything from chefs to China, but he focuses primarily on sports. Andrew is a lifelong fan of all sports, especially hockey. He lives in sunny Florida, where he enjoys spending time with his wife and kids.

CONTENTS

Go Blackhawks! . . . 4
Becoming the Blackhawks . . . 7
By the Numbers . . . 8
Game Night . . . 11
Uniforms . . . 12
Team Spirit . . . 15
Heroes of History . . . 16
Big Days . . . 18
Modern-Day Marvels . . . 20
The G.O.A.T. . . . 23
The Big Game . . . 24
Amazing Feats . . . 27
All-Time Best . . . 28

Glossary . . . 30
Fast Facts . . . 31
One Stride Further . . . 31
Find Out More . . . 32
Index . . . 32

Go Blackhawks!

The Chicago Blackhawks play in the National Hockey League's (NHL) Western Conference. The team is in the conference's Central Division. The Hawks, as the team is commonly known, have won six Stanley Cup championships in their history, which is tied with the Boston Bruins for the fourth-most ever. The Blackhawks' main division **rivals** are the St. Louis Blues. But their biggest rivalry in the league is with the Atlantic Division Detroit Red Wings.

Western Conference • Central Division

Chicago Blackhawks	**Dallas Stars**	**Nashville Predators**	**Utah Hockey Club**
Colorado Avalanche	**Minnesota Wild**	**St. Louis Blues**	**Winnipeg Jets**

Connor Bedard celebrates a goal with his teammates during a 2024 game against the Dallas Stars.

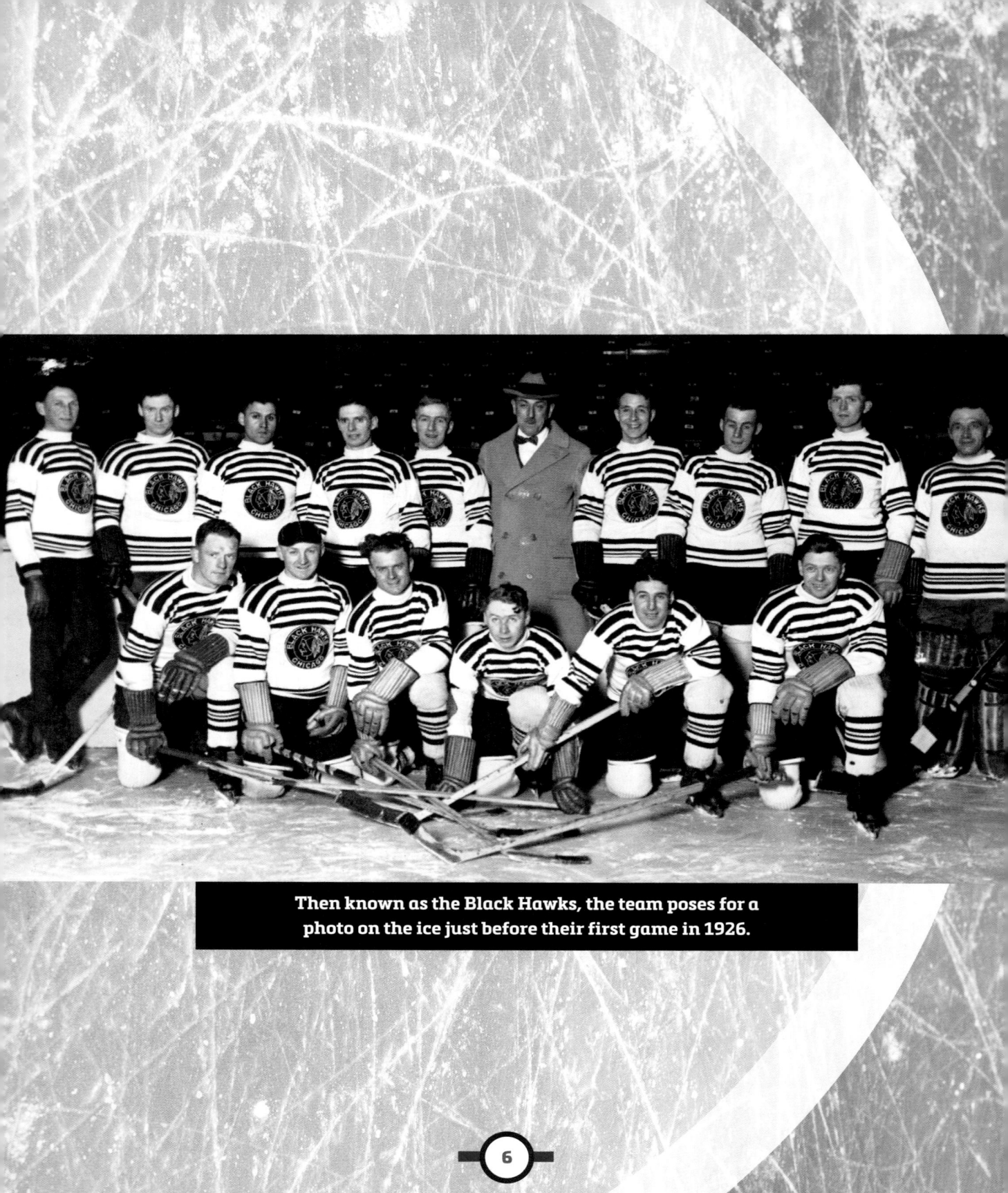

Then known as the Black Hawks, the team poses for a photo on the ice just before their first game in 1926.

Becoming the Blackhawks

The team entered the NHL as the Chicago Black Hawks for the 1926–1927 season. They changed Black Hawks to Blackhawks in 1986. The team is named for a World War I army battalion that was nicknamed the Blackhawks. The nickname came from a Sauk tribe leader named Chief Black Hawk.

Chicago had one main **dynasty** period in its history. In the 2010s, the Hawks won three Stanley Cups in six seasons. Led by the dynamic duo of captain and center Jonathan Toews (pronounced TAYVES) and **All-Star** winger Patrick Kane, the Blackhawks won the Cup in 2010, 2013, and 2015.

By the Numbers

 s an **Original Six** team, the Blackhawks have a long history that includes plenty of numbers to examine. Let's take a look:

 The Blackhawks have a great track record when they have the third overall pick in the NHL **Draft**. In 1980, they took Blackhawk legend Denis Savard, followed by Ed Olczyk (OLE-chek) in 1984 and longtime captain Jonathan Toews in 2006.

 Hall of Fame defenseman Pierre Pilote (Pee-LUTT) set a Black Hawk team record in 1966–1967 when he posted a 54 **plus/minus rating**.

 In 2009–2010, the Blackhawks won 52 games, the most wins in a single season for the team. They went on to win the Stanley Cup that season.

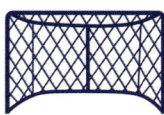 The Blackhawks have appeared in the playoffs 63 times. The team went all the way to the Stanley Cup Final in 13 of those appearances. **63**

Pierre Pilote played all but one season of his pro career with the Blackhawks. He scored 477 points, including 400 assists, for Chicago.

Chicago's United Center holds more than 20,000 hockey fans for home Blackhawks games.

Game Night

The Blackhawks played at the Chicago Coliseum for parts of the first three seasons, from 1926-1929. They played the next 65 seasons at the brand-new Chicago Stadium, known as "The Madhouse on Madison" because of their rowdy fans. In 1985, fans at the stadium started the tradition of cheering loudly during the playing of the national anthem. The tradition continues at the United Center, the team's home since 1994.

We're Famous!

The Blackhawks are a theme of the *Wayne's World* movies from the 1990s. The movies are set in the Chicago suburb of Aurora. The main characters, Wayne and Garth, appear wearing Blackhawks sweaters in several scenes. Also, the fictional donut shop in town is called Stan Mikita's Donuts, named for the Blackhawks superstar.

Uniforms

HOME

AWAY

Showing Respect

Goalie Marc-André Fleury is well-known around the league for having cool goalie mask designs. These designs are carefully chosen because they have meaning to him. Fleury played for the Blackhawks during the 2021–2022 season. In November of that season, he wore a special mask. November is Native American **Heritage** Month. The mask was designed by an artist from the Ojibwe tribe. It was all black with three colorful feathers painted on the forehead. Fleury, whose wife is of Native American descent, made sure the design was authentic to the Ojibwe heritage.

Truly Weird

A hat trick occurs when a player scores three goals in one game. Hat tricks are rare in hockey. The NHL's top hat trick-scorers might log between three and six in a whole season. But one Blackhawks player has a very unusual hat trick stat. During the last game of the 1951–1952 season, Chicago player Bill Mosienko scored three goals in just 21 seconds—the fastest hat trick in NHL history. The Blackhawks defeated the New York Rangers 7–6 that night thanks to Mosienko's quick work. Fans can see the pucks and stick from the "Mosienko Miracle" at the Hockey Hall of Fame museum in Canada.

Team Spirit

The Blackhawks' mascot is named Tommy Hawk. The team is named after Black Hawk, a Native American tribal chief. A tomahawk is a traditional Native American weapon. Tommy's costume looks like a common black hawk, a bird of prey in nature, wearing a Black Hawks uniform. Black hawks are rare in the United States, and Tommy might be the only one near Chicago. These birds only fly as far north as the Southwestern United States. As for Tommy, he can mostly be found at the United Center. His hobbies include spraying silly string, launching confetti and T-shirts, and dancing.

◀ When he's not flapping around on the ice at the United Center, Tommy Hawk appears in parades and shows up at schools, businesses, and hospitals in the Chicago area.

Heroes of History

Bobby Hull
Left Wing | 1957–1972

Twelve-time All-Star Bobby Hull played the first 15 seasons of his long career with the Blackhawks. Hull was known for his speed and his ability to put the puck in the net. He scored 604 goals for the Hawks and led the NHL in goals scored seven times. Hull won two league Most Valuable Player (MVP) awards, three league scoring titles, and one Stanley Cup. He became part of the Hockey Hall of Fame in 1983.

Patrick Kane
Right Wing | 2007–2023

The Blackhawks chose Buffalo, New York, native Patrick Kane with the first overall pick in the 2007 NHL Draft. Kane more than lived up to expectations. He had one of the most successful careers in team history. Kane started by winning **Rookie** of the Year in 2008. Kane's nickname was "Showtime." He was a key player in the team's three Stanley Cup wins in the 2010s, winning playoff MVP in 2013. The four-time All-Star also won an NHL MVP award in 2016 when he led the league in scoring.

Denis Savard
Center | 1980–1990, 1995–1997

Denis Savard may be the best all-around scorer in Hawks history. The former team captain had five 100-point seasons in his first eight years in the NHL. This included a career team record 131 points in 1988. Savard had three 40-goal seasons. He was known throughout the league for being an expert at the "Savardian Spin-O-Rama," a quick pivoting move used to get around a defender. Savard played in six All-Star games with Chicago.

Doug Wilson
Defenseman | 1977–1991

Some people will argue that there are other players who should have this spot on the list, but Doug Wilson deserves recognition for his outstanding Hall of Fame career. Wilson played 14 of his 16 NHL seasons in Chicago. In 1982, Wilson won the award as the best defenseman in the NHL. He leads the Hawks in career goals, assists, and points by a defenseman. Wilson played 938 games and six All-Star games as a Blackhawk.

Big Days

APRIL 12, 1938

Chicago beats Toronto 3–1 to win the Stanley Cup. The Hawks win the championship after winning just 14 regular-season games, the fewest ever by a Cup winner.

Bobby Hull scores his 600th career goal. The goal comes on the **power play** against Boston. Only 19 other players in NHL history have accomplished this feat.

MARCH 25, 1972

JUNE 22, 2007

With the first overall pick in the 2007 NHL Draft, Chicago takes high-scoring winger Patrick Kane. This pick is the building block of the teams that win three Cups.

The Blackhawks defeat Philadelphia 4–3 in **overtime** on a goal by Patrick Kane in Game 6 of the Stanley Cup Final. The win gives the team its first championship in 49 years.

JUNE 9, 2010

Modern-Day Marvels

Connor Bedard
Center | 2023–Present

Connor Bedard was one of the most-hyped **prospects** in NHL history. He was so much better than the other players that he got permission to play above his age group at 15. In his last season of junior hockey, Bedard scored 71 goals and 143 points in just 57 games playing against older players. The Blackhawks drafted him first overall in 2023. Bedard won Rookie of the Year in 2024. He is now the team's foundation as the Hawks rebuild around him.

Frank Nazar
Center | 2024–Present

Frank Nazar was Chicago's first round pick in the 2022 NHL Draft. Nazar made an exciting NHL debut for the Blackhawks on April 14, 2024. He wasted no time in showing off his skills. Nazar scored his first career goal on his very first shot in a 4–2 loss to the Carolina Hurricanes. Known for his blazing speed, Nazar's game is built on quickness. But he still has room to grow. Nazar is working on his talents as part of the US men's national junior hockey team. In 2024, he earned eight assists and helped lead the US to a gold medal at the World Junior Ice Hockey Championship. Blackhawks fans hope to see more of him on the ice in the future.

Artyom Levshunov
Defenseman | 2024–Present
Artyom Levshunov is the Blackhawks' top prospect—that means the team hopes he will play a big role on the team in the future. Chicago drafted the defenseman second overall in 2024. He was born and raised in Belarus but played one season at Michigan State, where he scored 35 points in just 38 games. Chicago fans are excited about Levshunov being the team's top defenseman for years to come.

Alex Vlasic
Defenseman | 2022–Present
The Blackhawks chose Alex Vlasic in the 2019 NHL Draft. He joined the team in 2022 after finishing his college hockey career at Boston University. In his first four seasons with the Blackhawks, Vlasic racked up 38 assists and scored six goals. The young defender has also been part of two US youth national hockey teams and the US men's national ice hockey team. His skills on the ice make him one of Chicago's top defenders as they hunt for another Stanley Cup win.

Stan Mikita is Chicago's all-time leader in several categories, including games played and career points.

The G.O.A.T.

When he was eight years old, Stan Mikita moved with his aunt and uncle from Czechoslovakia to Canada. That's where he learned to play hockey. When he turned 16, Mikita signed on to play with a **minor league** team near where he grew up. That team had connections to the Blackhawks. A few years later, Chicago called him up to the NHL, and he never looked back. Mikita went on to lead the league in scoring four times. He also won two MVP awards. In 1961, Mikita won his first and only Stanley Cup with the Blackhawks.

Fan Favorite

Defenseman Keith Magnuson was a big hit with the fans right away because he led the NHL in **penalty minutes** in his first two seasons. Magnuson was always willing to stick up for a teammate, and the fans loved him for it. Magnuson was the Blackhawks' captain during his last four seasons.

The Big Game

On May 30, 2015, Chicago faced the Anaheim Ducks in Game 7 of the Western Conference Final. The winner would move on to play for the Stanley Cup. The series had been a long one. There was an overtime game, a double overtime game, and a triple overtime game. That's like playing eight games instead of six! Chicago was determined to get back to the Final. They started fast in Game 7. The Hawks scored the first four goals of the game and won 5–3. Led by playoff MVP defenseman Duncan Keith, Chicago went on to win the last of its three Cups in six years.

Blackhawks players Patrick Kane, Brandon Saad, and Marcus Kruger celebrate their Game 7 win during the 2015 Western Conference Final.

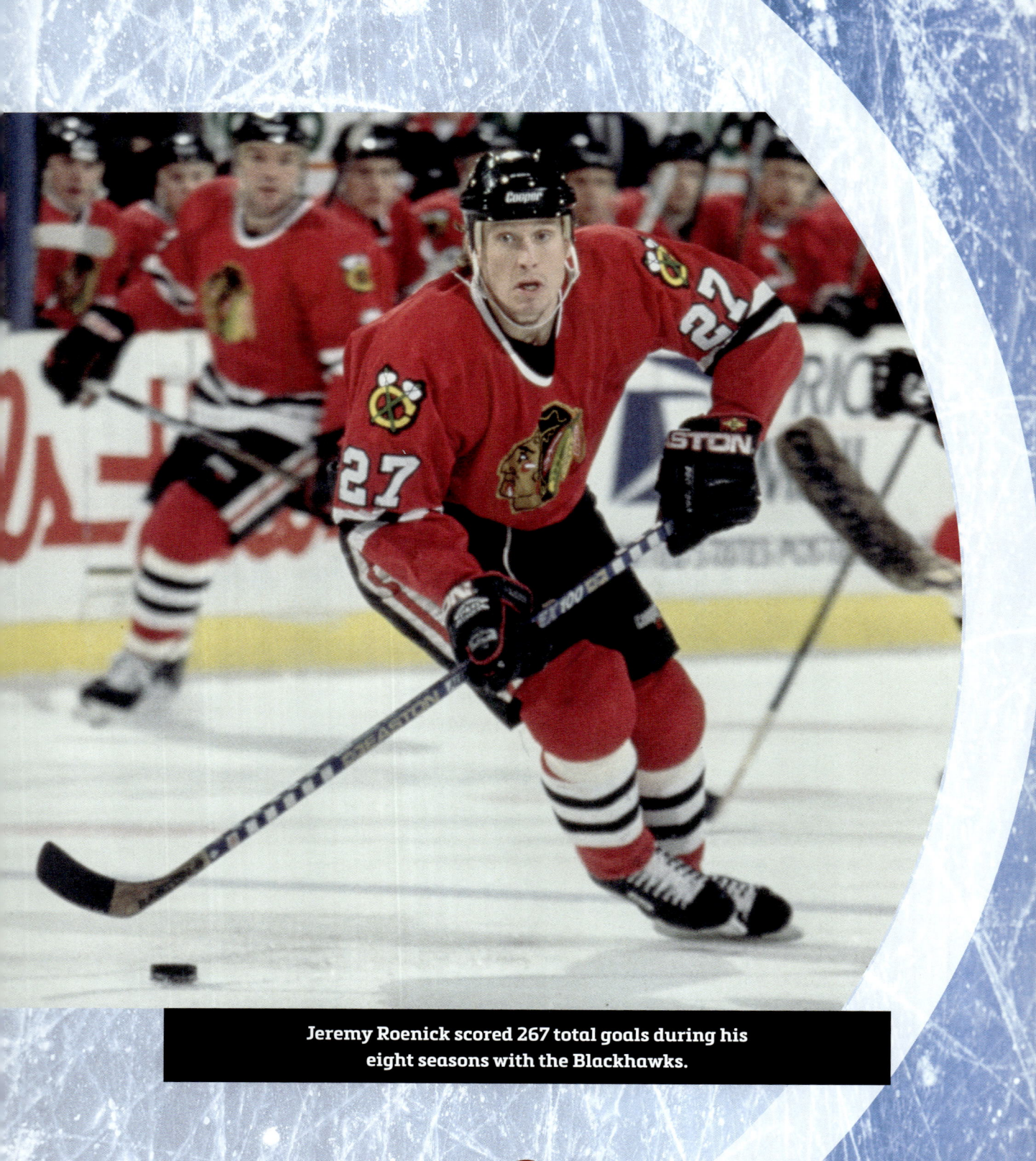
Jeremy Roenick scored 267 total goals during his eight seasons with the Blackhawks.

Amazing Feats

Shutouts
In 1969–1970, Blackhawks goaltender Tony Esposito set the team record for shutouts in a season when he held 15 opponents off of the scoresheet.

15

Penalty Minutes
Blackhawks winger Mike Peluso racked up a team record 408 penalty minutes in 1991–1992, which is also the third most in a season in NHL history.

408

Points by a Defenseman
Longtime Hawks defenseman Doug Wilson was also one of the team's best offensive players. He scored a team record 85 points in 1981–1982.

85

Power Play Goals
Hall of Fame center Jeremy Roenick was a great goal scorer for the Hawks from 1988 to 1996. In the 1993–1994 season, Roenick scored a team record 24 power play goals.

24

All-Time Best

MOST POINTS
1	Stan Mikita	1,467
2	Patrick Kane	1,225
3	Bobby Hull	1,153
4	Denis Savard	1,096
5	Steve Larmer	923

MOST HAT TRICKS
1	Bobby Hull	28
2	Stan Mikita	16
3	Denis Savard	11
4	Patrick Kane	9
	Steve Larmer	9

MOST GOALS
1	Bobby Hull	604
2	Stan Mikita	541
3	Patrick Kane	446
4	Steve Larmer	406
5	Denis Savard	377

MOST WINS
1	Tony Esposito	418
2	Glenn Hall	276
3	Corey Crawford	260
4	Ed Belfour	201
5	Jocelyn Thibault	137

MOST ASSISTS
1	Stan Mikita	926
2	Patrick Kane	779
3	Denis Savard	719
4	Doug Wilson	554
5	Bobby Hull	549

MOST SHUTOUTS
1	Tony Esposito	74
2	Glenn Hall	51
3	Charlie Gardiner	42
4	Ed Belfour	30
5	Mike Karakas	28
	Jocelyn Thibault	28

Tony Esposito made 24,378 saves for the Blackhawks over 15 seasons.

GLOSSARY

All-Star (ALL STAR) An All-Star is a player chosen as one of the best in their sport.

draft (DRAFT) A draft is a yearly event when teams take turns choosing new players. In the NHL, teams can select North American ice hockey players between the ages of 18 and 20 and international players between 18 and 21 to join the league.

dynasty (DYE-nuh-stee) A dynasty is a powerful group, such as a team, that leads or rules for a long period of time.

heritage (HAYR-uh-tij) Someone's heritage is a tradition or practice passed down through generations or within a culture.

minor league (MY-nor LEEG) A minor league is a professional league that is below a sport's top league. Young players often start in the minor league to gain valuable playing experience.

Original Six (oh-RIJ-uh-nul SIX) The Original Six were the teams that made up the NHL from 1942–1967. They were the Boston Bruins, Chicago Blackhawks, Detroit Red Wings, Montreal Canadiens, New York Rangers, and Toronto Maple Leafs.

overtime (OH-vur-tym) Overtime is extra time added to the end of a game when the regular time is up and the score is tied.

penalty minutes (PEN-ul-tee MIN-uhts) In hockey, penalty minutes or PIM is the total amount of time a player spends off the ice for committing fouls.

plus/minus rating (PLUS/MY-nus RAY-ting) Plus/minus rating is the measurement of how well the team scores when each player is on the ice.

power play (POW-uhr PLAY) A power play occurs when a player gets a penalty and the other team has more players on the ice.

prospect (PROS-pekt) A prospect is a player with the skills necessary to help a team succeed in the future.

rival (RYE-vuhl) A rival is a team's top competitor, which they try to outdo and play better than each season.

rookie (ROOK-ee) A rookie is a new or first-year player in a professional sport.

FAST FACTS

- Blackhawks star Connor Bedard thinks it is bad luck for anyone else to touch his stick before a game.

- Blackhawks defenseman Kevin Korchinski has talents outside of hockey. Korchinski plays the piano and the guitar.

- When Patrick Kane scored the winning goal in overtime to clinch the Blackhawks' Stanley Cup victory in 2010, he was only one of a few in the arena who saw the puck go in. He began throwing his gloves in the air and celebrating by himself before the goal was confirmed.

- The Blackhawks have retired nine uniform numbers belonging to 10 different players. Pierre Pilote and Keith Magnuson both wore the number three, and the team decided both were worthy of the honor.

ONE STRIDE FURTHER

- The Blackhawks have had two megastar eras. One was with Bobby Hull and Stan Mikita. The other was with Patrick Kane and Jonathan Toews. Which era do you think was more important in Hawks history? Make a chart showing your comparison.

- Chicago is one of the Original Six teams. Look up the other five teams. Where do you think the Blackhawks rank among those teams, and why?

- Make a top-10 list of the greatest players in Blackhawks history. How many of them played their whole career in Chicago? Does that make a difference when you rank the players?

- Hockey has been around for more than a century. Look up the history of hockey in Chicago. How did the sport get started, and what made it popular in Chicago?

FIND OUT MORE

IN THE LIBRARY

Bamford, Tab. *Chicago Blackhawks: An Illustrated Timeline*. St. Louis, MO: Reedy Press, 2020.

Bamford, Tab. *The Future: Connor Bedard and the Chicago Blackhawks' New Era*. Chicago, IL: Triumph Books, 2025.

Laughlin, Kara L. *Hockey*. Parker, CO: The Child's World, 2024.

ON THE WEB

Visit our website for links about the Chicago Blackhawks:
childsworld.com/links

Note to Parents, Caregivers, Teachers, and Librarians: We routinely verify our web links to make sure they are safe and active sites. So encourage your readers to check them out!

INDEX

Bedard, Connor 5, 20, 31

Central Division 4

Esposito, Tony 27–28

Fleury, Marc-André 13

Hull, Bobby 16, 18, 28, 31

Kane, Patrick 7, 16, 19, 24, 28, 31

Magnuson, Keith 23, 31

Mikita, Stan 11, 22–23, 28, 31

Pilote, Pierre 8, 31

Savard, Denis 8, 17, 28

Stanley Cup 4, 7–8, 16, 18–19, 23–24, 31

Tommy Hawk 15

United Center 10–11, 15

Wilson, Doug 17, 27–28

Made in the USA
Middletown, DE
10 April 2025

74097019R00029